Roma Travel Guide:

From Ancient Glories to Culinary Delights and Hidden Cultural Gems, Make Sure You Don't Miss Out on the Hidden Gems of the Italian Capital

Calliope Foster

Chapter 5 Roman Cuisine and Culinary Adventures 53

5.1 Traditional Roman Dishes 53

5.2 Food Markets 55

5.3 Wine Tasting in Rome 58

5.4 Gelato Hotspots 60

5.5 Cooking Classes 61

Chapter 6 Rome's Art and Culture Scene 64

6.1 Galleria Borghese 64

6.2 MAXXI - National Museum of 21st Century Arts 66

6.3 The Pantheon 68

6.4 Contemporary Art Galleries 71

6.5 Street Art in Rome 73

Chapter 7 Shopping and Fashion in Rome...............................76

7.1 Via Condotti 76

7.2 Campo Marzio 79

7.3 Vintage and Antique Shops 81

7.4 Roman Markets...84

7.5 Fashion Events and Festivals...87

Conclusion Practical Information and Final Thoughts 90

Chapter 1
Introduction to Roma

1.1 Welcome to Roma

Welcome to Roma, a city steeped in a rich tapestry of history, culture, and timeless allure. Nestled along the banks of the Tiber River, this ancient metropolis stands as a living testament to the grandeur of bygone eras.

At the heart of Rome lies its historical significance as the capital of the once-mighty Roman Empire. Founded in 753 BC, the city has witnessed the rise and fall of civilizations, and its streets and monuments echo with the footsteps of emperors, gladiators, and scholars.

The architectural marvels of Rome are a captivating blend of classical and Renaissance influences. The iconic Colosseum, a colossal amphitheater where gladiators once battled for glory, stands proudly as a symbol of Roman engineering prowess. Meanwhile, the Roman Forum, a sprawling archaeological complex, offers a glimpse into the political, religious, and commercial life of ancient Rome.

Beyond its ancient allure, modern Rome pulsates with vibrant energy. Wandering through the narrow cobblestone streets of districts like Trastevere, you'll discover a charming juxtaposition of medieval architecture and trendy boutiques. Cafés and trattorias beckon with the promise of delectable Roman cuisine, inviting you to savor the flavors of pasta, pizza, and other culinary delights.

Vatican City, an independent city-state nestled within Rome's embrace, is a spiritual and artistic epicenter. Home to St. Peter's Basilica and the Vatican Museums, this sovereign enclave encapsulates centuries of religious and artistic treasures. Michelangelo's awe-inspiring frescoes in the Sistine Chapel and the grandeur of St. Peter's Square are testaments to the city's enduring cultural legacy.

As you embark on your Roman adventure, prepare to be enchanted by the allure of the Eternal City. From the grandeur of ancient monuments to the vivacity of modern life, Rome unfolds its stories, inviting you to immerse yourself in a journey through time and culture. So, let the eternal charm of Roma captivate your senses and lead you through its enchanting streets and hidden gems. Welcome to a city where every cobblestone has a story to tell.

- Brief history and significance

Rome, a city with a history as vast as its influence, stands as a living testament to the evolution of civilization over millennia. Its origins date back to the legendary founding by Romulus in 753 BC, according to ancient mythology. Over the centuries, Rome grew from a small village on the banks of the Tiber River into the capital of one of the most powerful empires in history – the Roman Empire.

The rise of the Roman Empire marked a pivotal era in human history, spanning from 27 BC to 476 AD. During this time, Rome flourished as a center of politics, culture, and military might, reaching its zenith under emperors like Augustus, Nero, and Trajan. The Roman Empire left an indelible mark on the Western world, influencing governance, architecture, engineering, and law.

The city's significance extends beyond its imperial past. In the heart of Rome lies the Roman Forum, a sprawling archaeological site that served as the political, religious, and commercial center of ancient Rome. The Colosseum, an architectural marvel, hosted gladiatorial contests and grand spectacles, symbolizing the grandeur and entertainment of the time.

As the Western Roman Empire crumbled, Rome underwent transformations, transitioning from an imperial capital to a cultural and religious hub. In the 4th century, Christianity took root, and Rome became the seat of the Catholic Church. St. Peter's Basilica, situated in Vatican City, stands as a testament to this spiritual legacy.

Over the centuries, Rome experienced periods of decline, invasions, and revival during the Renaissance. The city's artistic and cultural reawakening gave birth to masterpieces like Michelangelo's Sistine Chapel ceiling and Raphael's frescoes in the Vatican Museums.

Today, Rome is a thriving metropolis that seamlessly blends its rich history with the demands of contemporary life. Its significance lies not only in its ancient ruins but also in its role as a global center for art, culture, and diplomacy. Whether wandering through the ruins of the Forum or marveling at the architectural prowess of the Pantheon, visitors are surrounded by the echoes of a city that has shaped the course of history for over two millennia. In every cobblestone and ancient structure, Rome's enduring significance is palpable, inviting all who explore its streets to partake in the unfolding narrative of this remarkable city.

1.2 Getting to Roma

- Transportation options

Getting to Roma is a journey marked by convenience and accessibility, offering a variety of transportation options that cater to diverse preferences and travel styles. Whether arriving by air, land, or sea, the Eternal City welcomes visitors with a network of well-connected and efficient transportation choices.

Air Travel: Rome is served by two major international airports:

1. Leonardo da Vinci-Fiumicino Airport (FCO):
   - Located about 30 kilometers southwest of the city center.
   - Italy's primary airport, offering a wide range of international flights.
   - Well-connected to the city by express trains, buses, and taxis.
2. Ciampino-G. B. Pastine International Airport (CIA):
   - Situated approximately 15 kilometers southeast of Rome.
   - Mainly serves low-cost and charter airlines.
   - Accessible by airport shuttle buses, taxis, and car rentals.

Train Travel: Rome's central location makes it easily accessible by train, offering efficient rail connections throughout Italy and Europe. The city is served by several major train stations, with Roma Termini being the primary hub for domestic and international routes.

1. Roma Termini:
   - Italy's largest train station.
   - Well-connected to major cities within Italy and neighboring countries.
   - High-speed trains, regional trains, and international services are available.

Bus and Coach Services: For those seeking a more economical travel option, long-distance buses and coaches provide a cost-effective and scenic journey to Rome.

1. Bus Terminals:
   - Various bus terminals, such as Tiburtina and EUR, serve different parts of the city.
   - Comfortable coaches link Rome to cities across Italy and Europe.

Car Travel: While traffic in Rome can be challenging, traveling by car offers flexibility and the opportunity to explore surrounding areas at your own pace.

1. Road Networks:
   - Italy boasts an extensive network of highways and well-maintained roads.
   - Car rentals are available at airports and throughout the city.

Cruise Travel: For those arriving by sea, Rome is accessible through the nearby port of Civitavecchia.

1. Civitavecchia Port:
   - Located approximately 80 kilometers northwest of Rome.
   - Cruise ships dock here, and transportation options include trains, buses, and private transfers to the city.

Navigating the transportation options to Roma is part of the adventure, allowing visitors to tailor their journey to suit their preferences and schedules. Whether soaring into Fiumicino, arriving by high-speed train at Termini, or taking a scenic bus ride, each mode of transport provides a unique introduction to the captivating city that awaits exploration.

- Airport information

Leonardo da Vinci-Fiumicino Airport, commonly known as Fiumicino Airport, serves as Rome's primary international airport. Located approximately 30 kilometers southwest of the city center, FCO is a major gateway to Italy and one of the busiest airports in Europe. Here is essential information for travelers arriving or departing from Fiumicino:

1. Terminals:
   - Fiumicino Airport has four terminals: T1, T2, T3, and T5.
   - T1 is primarily used for domestic flights, while T3 is the main terminal for international flights.
2. Transportation to/from the Airport:
   - **Train:** The Leonardo Express is a dedicated non-stop train service connecting Fiumicino Airport to Roma Termini, the main train station in Rome. The journey takes approximately 30 minutes.
   - **Bus:** Several bus services operate between the airport and various locations in Rome, providing a cost-effective transportation option.

- **Taxi:** Taxis are readily available outside the terminals. The journey to the city center takes around 45 minutes, depending on traffic.
- **Car Rental:** Numerous car rental agencies have counters at the airport, offering a convenient option for those planning to explore the region by car.

3. Services and Amenities:
   - Fiumicino Airport provides a wide range of services, including currency exchange, ATMs, shopping outlets, and duty-free stores.
   - Dining options encompass traditional Italian cuisine, international dishes, and quick bites.
   - Lounges are available for passengers seeking a more comfortable and private environment.

4. Flight Information:
   - The airport operates flights to and from destinations worldwide, connecting Rome to major cities across Europe, the Americas, Asia, and Africa.
   - Flight information, including arrivals and departures, can be accessed through the airport's website or information boards within the terminals.

5. COVID-19 Measures:
   - As of my last knowledge update in January 2022, COVID-19 measures may be in place, including health screenings, testing facilities, and mask mandates. Travelers are advised to check the latest travel advisories and airport guidelines.

Fiumicino Airport, named after the renowned Italian polymath Leonardo da Vinci, serves as a modern and efficient entry point to Rome, ensuring a smooth transition for both leisure and business travelers.

1.3 Essential Travel Tips

- Currency and language

Welcome to the enchanting city of Rome, where history, art, and culinary delights converge to create an unforgettable travel experience. As you embark on your Roman adventure, familiarizing yourself with essential travel tips, particularly regarding currency and language, will enhance your exploration of this timeless destination.

Currency:

Euro (EUR): Rome operates on the Euro (EUR), the official currency of Italy. It's advisable to have some Euros on hand for smaller expenses, such as street vendors or local markets, where card payments might not be as common. Currency exchange services are readily available at airports, banks, and currency exchange offices throughout the city.

Credit Cards: Credit cards are widely accepted in most establishments, including hotels, restaurants, and shops. However, it's recommended to inform your bank about your travel dates to avoid any unexpected issues. Ensure your card is compatible with European chip and PIN technology.

ATMs: ATMs are conveniently located across Rome, allowing you to withdraw Euros as needed. Be aware of any international withdrawal fees your bank may charge, and keep in mind that using ATMs affiliated with major banks can often minimize these fees.

Small Change: Keeping small denominations of Euros is practical for various situations, including tipping at restaurants and cafes. This practice ensures smooth transactions, particularly in places where making change for larger bills might be challenging.

Language:

Italian Language: Italian is the official language of Rome, and while English is widely spoken in tourist areas, making an effort to learn basic Italian phrases can enhance your interactions and show appreciation for the local culture.

Common Phrases: Learning a few common phrases such as "Grazie" (Thank you) and "Per favore" (Please) can go a long way. Locals appreciate visitors attempting the local language, fostering a sense of connection and cultural understanding.

Language Apps: Consider using language apps to familiarize yourself with essential Italian phrases. These tools can be invaluable for navigating day-to-day interactions and enriching your travel experience.

English in Tourist Areas: In major tourist hubs, English is widely used, and you'll find information signs, menus, and staff proficient in the language. However, venturing into more local neighborhoods may require a bit more reliance on basic Italian.

Cultural Etiquette: Immerse yourself in the local culture by respecting customs and traditions. Dress modestly when visiting religious sites, and engage in polite greetings. Italians are known for their warmth, and a friendly "Buongiorno" can open doors to memorable interactions.

Additional Tips:

Cultural Sensitivity: Respect local customs and traditions, particularly when visiting religious sites or participating in cultural events. This cultural sensitivity fosters positive interactions and enriches your travel experience.

Emergency Services: Familiarize yourself with emergency numbers. In Italy, the general emergency number is 112. Additionally, the emergency medical services number is 118. Understanding these numbers ensures you're prepared in case of unexpected situations.

Adapters and Voltage: Italy uses the Europlug (Type C and F) electrical outlet. Ensure you have the necessary adapters for your devices, and check if your electronics can handle the 230V voltage.

Public Transportation Information: Learn about Rome's public transportation system, including buses and the metro. Understanding the city's public transport options will empower you to navigate efficiently, allowing you to explore the city's diverse neighborhoods and attractions seamlessly.

As you embark on your Roman journey, these travel tips will serve as your compass, guiding you through the city's rich tapestry of history, culture, and vibrant contemporary life. Enjoy every moment as you immerse yourself in the timeless charm of Rome.

- Local customs and etiquette

In the heart of Rome beats a cultural rhythm, shaped by centuries of history, tradition, and the warmth of its people. As you explore the Eternal City, understanding and embracing local customs and etiquette will not only enrich your experience but also allow you to connect more deeply with the captivating spirit of Rome.

1. Greetings and Politeness: Romans value politeness and courtesy in social interactions. When entering shops, restaurants, or other public spaces, a warm "Buongiorno" (Good morning) or "Buonasera" (Good evening) is customary. Adding "Per favore" (Please) and "Grazie" (Thank you) to your vocabulary goes a long way in demonstrating respect.

2. Dining Etiquette: Dining in Rome is a delightful experience filled with culinary delights and social engagement. Here are some dining etiquette tips:

- *Seating:* Wait to be seated in restaurants, especially in more formal settings.
- *Tipping:* A service charge is often included, but leaving small change or rounding up the bill is appreciated. In cafes, it's customary to leave small change on the counter.
- *Wine Tasting:* If invited to someone's home, a small gift, such as a bottle of wine, is a thoughtful gesture.

3. Dress Modestly, Especially at Religious Sites: When visiting churches and religious sites, dress modestly. Both men and women should cover shoulders and knees. Carrying a scarf or shawl can be helpful for impromptu visits to religious places.

4. Time and Punctuality: Romans have a more relaxed attitude toward time compared to some other cultures, but it's still essential to be reasonably punctual, especially for scheduled appointments and tours. Allow some flexibility and embrace the unhurried pace of life.

5. Public Behavior: In public spaces, maintain a level of decorum. Avoid loud conversations, especially in historical or religious sites. Romans appreciate a sense of tranquility and respect for the cultural significance of their surroundings.

6. Language Courtesy: While English is widely spoken in tourist areas, making an effort to speak Italian, even if just a few basic phrases, is appreciated. Romans respond warmly to visitors who show an interest in their language and culture.

7. Gestures and Expressions: Hand gestures are a common part of Italian communication. While many gestures are innocuous, it's advisable to be mindful of their context to avoid misunderstandings. For instance, a quick nod upward signifies agreement.

8. Queuing and Personal Space: Queuing in an orderly fashion is expected, especially in crowded places. Respect personal space and be mindful of others in public transport, queues, and crowded areas.

9. Celebrating Festivities: If you have the opportunity to experience local festivals or events, do so with respect and enthusiasm. Italians are proud of their traditions, and participating in local celebrations can provide unique insights into their cultural heritage.

10. Saying Goodbye: When bidding farewell, a simple "Arrivederci" (Goodbye) or "Ciao" is appropriate. If you've formed a connection with someone, consider a double-cheek kiss, which is a common and friendly gesture among friends.

By embracing these local customs and etiquette, you not only show respect for the traditions of Rome but also open doors to warm interactions and a more authentic experience in this captivating city. Enjoy your time in Rome, where every gesture and tradition is a step into the rich tapestry of Italian culture.

1.4 Weather and Best Time to Visit

Rome, with its timeless allure and historical treasures, beckons travelers throughout the year. To make the most of your visit to the Eternal City, understanding its climate and choosing the optimal time to explore is key. Let's delve into the climate overview and discover the best times to experience the enchantment of Rome.

1. Mediterranean Climate: Rome enjoys a Mediterranean climate, characterized by hot, dry summers and mild, wet winters. This climate pattern infuses the city with a pleasant ambiance throughout much of the year, making it an attractive destination for a variety of travelers.

2. Seasons:

- Summer (June to August):
    - Summer in Rome is characterized by high temperatures and an abundance of sunshine.
    - Average daytime temperatures range from 28°C to 32°C (82°F to 90°F).
    - This is the peak tourist season, with vibrant street life, festivals, and extended opening hours for attractions.
- Autumn (September to November):
    - Autumn brings milder temperatures and a more relaxed atmosphere.
    - Daytime temperatures range from 18°C to 25°C (64°F to 77°F).
    - This season offers a pleasant blend of warm weather and fewer crowds.
- Winter (December to February):
    - Winters in Rome are mild, with occasional rainfall.
    - Daytime temperatures range from 10°C to 15°C (50°F to 59°F).
    - While it's the low season for tourism, the city is adorned with festive lights during the holiday season.
- Spring (March to May):
    - Spring is a delightful time to visit, with blooming flowers and moderate temperatures.
    - Daytime temperatures range from 15°C to 23°C (59°F to 73°F).

- This season offers a perfect balance of comfortable weather and burgeoning greenery.

3. Best Time to Visit:

- The best time to visit Rome largely depends on personal preferences and the type of experience you seek.
- High Season (Late Spring to Early Fall):
    - Late spring (April to June) and early fall (September to October) are considered the best times to visit.
    - Mild temperatures, blooming flowers, and a lively atmosphere make these months ideal for sightseeing.
- Shoulder Seasons:
    - Late fall (November) and early spring (March) offer pleasant weather with fewer crowds.
    - This is an excellent time for exploring attractions without the summer hustle.
- Low Season (Winter):
    - While winters are mild, some attractions may have shorter opening hours, and outdoor activities may be limited.
    - However, the city takes on a serene charm, and accommodations may be more affordable.

4. Considerations:

- Rome's peak tourist season coincides with the summer months, so expect larger crowds at popular attractions and higher prices for accommodations.
- If you prefer a quieter experience and can tolerate slightly cooler temperatures, the shoulder seasons provide a wonderful balance between comfortable weather and fewer visitors.
- Keep in mind that weather conditions can vary, and it's advisable to check the forecast closer to your travel dates.

Rome's climate invites exploration year-round, each season offering a unique perspective on this historic city. Whether basking in the summer sun, strolling through autumnal gardens, or enjoying the mild winter ambiance, Rome awaits with its timeless charm and cultural treasures. Choose the season that aligns with your preferences, and let the Eternal City captivate you.

- Ideal months for travel

Embarking on a journey to Rome is a delightful venture into history, culture, and timeless charm. To ensure your experience is nothing short of magical, choosing the ideal months for your visit is essential. Let's explore the nuances of each season to help you pinpoint the perfect time to wander through the cobblestone streets and ancient wonders of the Eternal City.

1. Late Spring (April to June):

- *Temperature:* Daytime temperatures range from 15°C to 23°C (59°F to 73°F).
- *Atmosphere:* Late spring is a golden period when the city bursts into bloom. The weather is comfortably warm, and outdoor cafes beckon with the promise of la dolce vita.
- *Events:* This season is ideal for cultural events and festivals, with many outdoor activities and extended opening hours for attractions.
- *Crowds:* While more crowded than winter, it's generally less busy than the peak summer months.

2. Early Fall (September to October):

- *Temperature:* Daytime temperatures range from 18°C to 25°C (64°F to 77°F).
- *Atmosphere:* As summer wanes, early fall offers a delightful blend of warm days and cooler evenings. It's a time when the city is bathed in soft sunlight, creating a romantic ambiance.
- *Events:* Cultural events continue into the fall, and outdoor spaces remain inviting for leisurely exploration.
- *Crowds:* While still popular, the crowds tend to thin compared to the summer months.

3. Late Fall (November):

- *Temperature:* Daytime temperatures range from 10°C to 15°C (50°F to 59°F).
- *Atmosphere:* Late fall brings a crispness to the air and a quieter ambiance. The city takes on a serene charm, and autumnal colors paint the parks and historic streets.
- *Events:* While fewer major events occur, this is an excellent time for a more relaxed exploration of indoor attractions.
- *Crowds:* Fewer tourists make for a quieter experience at many popular sites.

4. Early Spring (March):

- *Temperature:* Daytime temperatures range from 10°C to 16°C (50°F to 61°F).
- *Atmosphere:* Early spring marks the awakening of the city. Trees blossom, and outdoor spaces begin to stir with life. It's an excellent time for those seeking milder temperatures.
- *Events:* Spring events commence, and the city gradually comes to life after the winter months.
- *Crowds:* While not as crowded as late spring, some attractions may still see moderate visitation.

Considerations:

- Summer (July to August):
    - While summer brings warmth and long daylight hours, it is the peak tourist season. Expect higher temperatures, larger crowds, and increased prices for accommodations.
- Winter (December to February):
    - Winters are mild, but some attractions may have reduced hours. If you prefer a quieter experience and are open to indoor explorations, winter can offer a more intimate encounter with the city.
- Year-Round Attractions:
    - Rome's timeless landmarks, museums, and historical sites are accessible throughout the year. The Colosseum, Roman

Forum, and Vatican City remain iconic highlights, regardless of the season.

Selecting the ideal months for your visit to Rome depends on your preferences, whether you seek the vibrant energy of spring, the warmth of summer, the romantic ambiance of fall, or the tranquility of winter. Whichever season captures your heart, Rome is sure to leave an indelible mark on your soul.

1.5 Top Attractions Overview

Rome, the Eternal City, invites you on a captivating journey through history, culture, and architectural splendor. As you embark on this adventure, let's explore the must-see landmarks that define the essence of Rome, setting the stage for an enchanting exploration of the city's timeless wonders.

1. The Colosseum:

- *Icon of Ancient Rome:* The Colosseum stands as an iconic symbol of ancient Roman engineering and grandeur. This colossal amphitheater once hosted gladiatorial contests and public spectacles, embodying the spirit of ancient entertainment.

2. Roman Forum:

- *Historical Heart:* The Roman Forum, a vast archaeological complex, serves as the historical heart of Rome. It was the epicenter of ancient Roman public life, featuring temples, government buildings, and monuments that provide a glimpse into the city's vibrant past.

3. Vatican City and St. Peter's Basilica:

- *Spiritual and Artistic Epitome:* Vatican City, an independent city-state within Rome, is home to St. Peter's Basilica and the Vatican Museums. St. Peter's Basilica, with its stunning dome and Michelangelo's Pieta, stands as a masterpiece of Renaissance architecture and art.

4. The Pantheon:

- *Architectural Marvel:* The Pantheon, a temple turned church, showcases the architectural prowess of ancient Rome. Its iconic dome and oculus create a celestial ambiance, making it a testament to Roman engineering and an enduring symbol of celestial beauty.

5. Trevi Fountain:

- *Baroque Splendor:* The Trevi Fountain is a masterpiece of Baroque art, portraying the sea god Neptune surrounded by tritons and seahorses. Legend has it that tossing a coin over your shoulder into the fountain ensures your return to Rome, a tradition followed by countless visitors.

6. Spanish Steps and Piazza di Spagna:

- *Elegant Gathering Place:* The Spanish Steps, a grand staircase, lead to the charming Piazza di Spagna. This area is a beloved spot for locals and visitors alike, offering a picturesque setting for leisurely strolls and people-watching.

7. Piazza Navona:

- *Architectural Gem:* Piazza Navona is a stunning square adorned with fountains, including Bernini's masterpiece, the Fountain of the Four Rivers. This lively space is surrounded by cafes and showcases the splendor of Roman Baroque architecture.

8. Sistine Chapel:

- *Artistic Marvel:* Housed within the Vatican Museums, the Sistine Chapel is a pinnacle of Western art. Michelangelo's breathtaking frescoes, including The Last Judgment and the iconic ceiling, make this sacred space a testament to artistic genius.

Setting the Stage for Your Exploration: These landmarks represent just a glimpse into the wealth of treasures awaiting you in Rome. As you turn the pages of this guide, immerse yourself in the rich narratives, hidden gems, and practical insights that will enrich your journey through the Eternal City. From the echoes of gladiator battles in the Colosseum to the sublime beauty of the Sistine Chapel, Rome unveils its wonders for those ready to explore its timeless embrace. Buon viaggio! (Safe travels!)

Chapter 2
Exploring Ancient Rome

2.1 The Colosseum

The Colosseum, an imposing amphitheater standing as an enduring symbol of ancient Rome, narrates tales of gladiatorial combat, grand spectacles, and the pulse of a once-thriving empire.

History: Constructed under Emperor Vespasian of the Flavian dynasty, the Colosseum, also known as the Flavian Amphitheatre, was inaugurated in AD 80. It could accommodate over 50,000 spectators who gathered to witness a variety of public entertainments, including gladiator contests, animal hunts, and mock sea battles. The Colosseum reflects the architectural brilliance of ancient Rome, showcasing a groundbreaking use of arches, columns, and concrete.

Throughout its history, the Colosseum has withstood earthquakes, fires, and pillaging, yet it endures as an awe-inspiring testament to Roman engineering and innovation. Today, it stands as one of the most visited and iconic landmarks in the world.

Architecture: The Colosseum's architecture epitomizes the grandeur of Roman engineering. This elliptical amphitheater measures 189 meters in length, 156 meters in width, and 50 meters in height, with a complex system of vaults and corridors beneath the arena floor. The exterior features a series of arches, each adorned with decorative columns, showcasing the classical orders of architecture – Doric, Ionic, and Corinthian. The seating tiers, once divided among social classes, offer a glimpse into the hierarchical structure of Roman society.

The arena floor, originally covered with sand, could be flooded for naval battles or used to stage various events. The Colosseum's sheer scale and ingenious design showcase the Romans' architectural prowess, creating a spectacle that transcends time.

Tips for Visiting:

1. **Guided Tours:** Consider joining a guided tour to gain in-depth insights into the Colosseum's history and architecture. Knowledgeable guides bring the ancient arena to life with stories of gladiators, emperors, and the vibrant spectacles that unfolded within its walls.
2. **Ticket Options:** Purchase tickets in advance to avoid long lines, especially during peak tourist seasons. Consider combination tickets that also grant access to the Roman Forum and Palatine Hill, creating a comprehensive historical experience.
3. **Visit Early or Late:** To beat the crowds and enjoy a more serene experience, plan your visit early in the morning or later in

the afternoon. The soft sunlight during these times enhances the Colosseum's mystique.

4. **Comfortable Footwear:** The Colosseum involves a fair amount of walking, including stairs and uneven surfaces. Wear comfortable footwear to explore the amphitheater comfortably.

5. **Water and Sun Protection:** Rome's climate can be warm, especially in summer. Carry water to stay hydrated, and use sunscreen and a hat to protect yourself from the sun.

6. **Photography:** Capture the grandeur of the Colosseum, but be mindful of any guidelines regarding flash photography or tripods. Respect the historical site by adhering to photography regulations.

7. **Audio Guides:** If a guided tour isn't your preference, consider using audio guides to enhance your visit. These guides provide informative commentary as you explore at your own pace.

As you step into the shadows of the Colosseum, envision the echoes of ancient roars, the cheers of the Roman populace, and the theatrical grandeur that once unfolded within its mighty walls. The Colosseum remains a living testament to the prowess of a civilization that left an indelible mark on the course of human history.

2.2 Roman Forum

The Roman Forum, nestled in the heart of ancient Rome, is a sprawling archaeological site that served as the bustling center of political, social, and religious life. As you wander through its ruins, envision the once vibrant marketplace and civic space that bore witness to the ebb and flow of Roman history.

Significance: The Roman Forum, or Forum Romanum, holds unparalleled historical significance as the nucleus of ancient Rome. It evolved from a marketplace into a hub of political and religious activities, surrounded by temples, basilicas, and government buildings. It was a place where citizens gathered for public speeches, elections, and ceremonies, shaping the destiny of the Roman Republic and later the Roman Empire.

Key Structures:

1. **Temple of Saturn:** Dedicated to the Roman god Saturn, this temple housed the state treasury and symbolized the wealth and stability of Rome.
2. **Arch of Septimius Severus:** Commemorating the victories of Emperor Septimius Severus and his sons, this triumphal arch stands as a testament to Rome's military might.
3. **Basilica Julia:** A grand judicial building where legal matters were conducted, reflecting the Roman emphasis on law and justice.
4. **Curia Julia:** The Senate House, where the Roman Senate convened to deliberate on matters of state. The current structure dates back to the reign of Julius Caesar.
5. **Temple of Vesta and House of the Vestal Virgins:** Dedicated to the goddess Vesta, this temple and the adjacent house were integral to the worship of the sacred fire tended by the Vestal Virgins.
6. **Arch of Titus:** Celebrating the military victories of Emperor Titus, this arch is renowned for its intricate reliefs depicting the spoils of the Siege of Jerusalem.
7. **Rostra:** A platform adorned with the prows of captured ships, used for public speeches and announcements. The term "rostrum" in modern language originates from this structure.

Guided Tour Suggestions:

1. Comprehensive Forum and Palatine Hill Tour:
   - Opt for a guided tour that includes the Roman Forum and Palatine Hill for a comprehensive exploration of Rome's historical center. This combination offers insights into the city's political, social, and imperial dimensions.
2. Archaeological Experts:
   - Engage with tours led by knowledgeable guides or archaeologists who can provide detailed historical context and bring the ancient structures to life with vivid narratives.
3. Early Morning or Evening Tours:
   - Consider scheduling your guided tour early in the morning or later in the evening to avoid the crowds and experience the Roman Forum in a more tranquil atmosphere.
4. Customizable Tours:

- Choose tours that allow some flexibility, enabling you to delve deeper into specific areas of interest within the Roman Forum based on your preferences.
5. Audio Guides:
   - If a guided tour is not your preference, audio guides are an excellent alternative. These provide informative commentary as you explore at your own pace.

Visiting the Roman Forum is akin to stepping back in time, where the whispers of ancient civilizations echo through the ruins. Guided tours offer a curated journey through this archaeological marvel, unveiling the layers of history that have shaped the destiny of Rome. As you stand amidst the remnants of ancient structures, let the stories of the Forum transport you to a bygone era.

2.3 Palatine Hill

Palatine Hill, one of the Seven Hills of Rome, stands as a testament to opulence, power, and the grandeur of imperial Rome. As you ascend this historic hill, prepare to be captivated by the remnants of lavish palaces and sprawling gardens that once graced the residences of emperors.

Imperial Palaces:

1. **Domus Flavia and Domus Augustana:** These imperial palaces served as the official residences of emperors, showcasing luxurious living quarters, reception rooms, and opulent courtyards. The Domus Flavia was built under Emperor Domitian, while the Domus Augustana was added by later emperors.
2. **Hippodrome of Domitian:** Originally an open space used for athletic competitions, the Hippodrome later transformed into a garden with a stadium and a water basin.
3. **Farnese Gardens:** Renaissance gardens created in the 16th century, offering a serene escape with panoramic views of Rome.
4. **Stadium of Domitian:** An ancient stadium used for athletic contests and, later, as a garden with walking paths and a central pool.

As you explore the archaeological wonders of Palatine Hill, imagine the vibrant life that once thrived within these palaces and gardens, shaping the destiny of the Roman Empire.

Views of the City:

The summit of Palatine Hill provides breathtaking panoramic views of Rome, offering a perspective that encompasses the city's iconic landmarks and its sprawling urban landscape.

1. **Circus Maximus:** From Palatine Hill, gaze upon the expansive Circus Maximus, once a chariot racing stadium and the largest entertainment venue in ancient Rome.
2. **Roman Forum:** Enjoy an elevated view of the Roman Forum, the heart of ancient Roman civic life, with its temples, basilicas, and iconic structures.
3. **Colosseum:** The Colosseum, an iconic symbol of ancient Rome, stands majestically in the distance, inviting contemplation of its historical significance.
4. **Capitoline Hill and Museums:** The neighboring Capitoline Hill and its museums, designed by Michelangelo, add another layer of historical richness to the panoramic vista.
5. **Dome of St. Peter's Basilica:** On a clear day, catch a glimpse of the dome of St. Peter's Basilica in Vatican City, connecting the ancient and Renaissance periods in one sweeping view.

Tips for Visiting:

1. **Combined Ticket:** Purchase a combined ticket that includes access to the Roman Forum, Palatine Hill, and the Colosseum. This ticket provides a comprehensive exploration of ancient Rome's historical center.
2. **Comfortable Footwear:** Palatine Hill involves walking on uneven terrain, so wear comfortable footwear to navigate the archaeological site comfortably.

3. **Guided Tours:** Engage in guided tours for a deeper understanding of the historical context, stories, and significance of the structures on Palatine Hill.
4. **Sun Protection:** Since Palatine Hill is an open-air archaeological site, bring sunscreen, a hat, and water to stay protected from the sun.
5. **Quiet Retreat:** Take a moment to appreciate the tranquility of the Farnese Gardens, offering a peaceful retreat amidst the ancient ruins.

Palatine Hill, with its regal ruins and sweeping views, invites you to unravel the layers of Roman history. As you wander through the remnants of imperial palaces and gaze upon the city below, feel the echoes of a bygone era reverberate through the centuries, making Palatine Hill an essential chapter in the story of Rome.

2.4 Capitoline Museums

Nestled atop Capitoline Hill, the Capitoline Museums stand as a cultural bastion, preserving and showcasing the artistic brilliance of ancient Rome. Here, visitors are treated to a captivating journey through time, exploring a rich collection of sculptures, artifacts, and masterpieces that encapsulate the essence of Rome's cultural and historical legacy.

Highlights:

1. **Capitoline Wolf:** A symbol of Rome, the Capitoline Wolf is an iconic bronze sculpture depicting a she-wolf suckling the legendary twins, Romulus and Remus.
2. **Marble Statue of Marcus Aurelius:** A majestic equestrian statue of the Roman Emperor Marcus Aurelius, celebrated for its exceptional craftsmanship and depiction of imperial power.
3. **Dying Gaul:** This poignant Hellenistic sculpture portrays a dying Gaul warrior, a powerful testament to the artistic and emotional depth of ancient Roman art.
4. **Capitoline Venus:** An exquisite marble sculpture representing the goddess Venus, showcasing the idealized beauty and grace that characterized Roman statuary.

5. **Ancient Roman Inscriptions and Reliefs:** The museums house an extensive collection of inscriptions, reliefs, and artifacts that offer insights into everyday life, politics, and religion in ancient Rome.

Visitor Information:

1. **Location:** The Capitoline Museums are located on Capitoline Hill, one of the Seven Hills of Rome. The complex consists of three buildings: Palazzo Senatorio, Palazzo dei Conservatori, and Palazzo Nuovo.
2. **Opening Hours:** The museums are typically open to the public throughout the week, with specific hours of operation. It's advisable to check the official website or contact the museum for the latest information on opening times.
3. **Tickets:** Visitors can purchase tickets on-site or online, with various ticket options available, including combined tickets with other Roman attractions. Consider guided tours for a more immersive experience.
4. **Guided Tours:** Engage in guided tours offered by the museums to gain deeper insights into the artworks and historical context. Knowledgeable guides provide valuable commentary, enriching your understanding of the exhibits.
5. **Accessibility:** The museums are committed to providing access to all visitors. Check for information regarding accessibility features, such as ramps and elevators, to ensure a comfortable visit.
6. **Temporary Exhibitions:** In addition to the permanent collection, the museums host temporary exhibitions, featuring rotating displays of art and artifacts. Check the schedule for any special exhibitions during your visit.
7. **Photography:** Review the museum's photography policy. While some areas may permit photography, others may have restrictions to protect delicate artifacts.
8. **Cafes and Amenities:** Explore the on-site cafes or nearby eateries for a refreshing break during your visit. Additionally,

find out about available amenities, such as restrooms and gift shops.

The Capitoline Museums beckon art enthusiasts, history buffs, and curious minds to immerse themselves in the splendor of ancient Rome. With its remarkable collection, the museum offers a profound encounter with the cultural tapestry that shaped the city and the world. As you explore the galleries, prepare to be transported to a time when art flourished, emperors ruled, and the echoes of ancient voices resonated through the Eternal City.

2.5 Circus Maximus

Circus Maximus, an ancient Roman chariot racing venue, stands as an expansive testament to the grandeur of public entertainment in ancient Rome. This historic site, nestled between the Palatine and Aventine Hills, once hosted thrilling chariot races that captivated the hearts of the Roman populace.

Historical Significance:

1. **Chariot Races:** Circus Maximus was the largest and most renowned circus in ancient Rome, capable of accommodating over 150,000 spectators. Chariot races, a beloved and iconic form of entertainment, took center stage, drawing fervent cheers and passionate support from the crowds.
2. **Obelisks and Decorations:** The spina, a central barrier within the circus, was adorned with Egyptian obelisks, statues, and other decorative elements. These embellishments added to the splendor of the races and provided a focal point for spectators.
3. **Cultural Gatherings:** Beyond chariot races, Circus Maximus hosted various public events, including religious ceremonies, processions, and triumphal parades celebrating military victories.

Present-Day Uses and Events:

While the grandeur of ancient chariot races is a distant memory, Circus Maximus has evolved to serve modern-day purposes, becoming a space for cultural events and public gatherings.

The chapel's simple yet elegant design ensures that attention is drawn to the artistic wonders adorning its walls and ceiling.

3. Fresco Restoration:
   - The restoration efforts in the late 20th century unveiled the original vibrancy of Michelangelo's colors, dispelling centuries of accumulated grime and soot. The restored frescoes now shine in their intended glory.

Visitor Etiquette:

The Sistine Chapel, a sacred space for both art and religion, requires visitors to observe certain etiquette to maintain its sanctity and preserve the artwork.

1. Silence and Reverence:
   - Maintain a respectful silence while inside the Sistine Chapel. This reverence is crucial to creating an atmosphere where visitors can fully appreciate the spiritual and artistic significance of the space.
2. No Photography or Talking:
   - Photography is strictly prohibited in the Sistine Chapel to preserve the frescoes. Visitors are also requested not to talk loudly. Guides often provide information outside the chapel to avoid disturbing the tranquil ambiance within.
3. Appropriate Attire:
   - As the Sistine Chapel is within the Vatican City, visitors are expected to dress modestly. Shoulders and knees should be covered, and hats should be removed as a sign of respect.
4. No Flash Photography:
   - Even if photography were allowed, the use of flash is strictly forbidden, as it can cause damage to the delicate pigments of the frescoes.
5. Stay within Designated Areas:
   - Visitors are required to stay within the designated areas and not touch the frescoes or architectural elements. The preservation of these masterpieces is paramount.
6. Chapel Exit:

- The Sistine Chapel has a designated exit leading directly to St. Peter's Basilica. If you wish to visit the basilica, you can use this exit without having to return to the Vatican Museums.
7. Timing Your Visit:
   - Consider visiting the Sistine Chapel during off-peak hours to experience a more serene atmosphere. Early mornings or late afternoons may offer a quieter setting compared to peak tourist hours.
8. Guided Tours:
   - Engaging in a guided tour can enhance your understanding of the artwork and its historical context. Guides often share insights that enrich the visitor experience.

As you step into the hallowed space of the Sistine Chapel, let the celestial beauty of Michelangelo's frescoes unfold before you. By respecting the sacredness of the chapel and adhering to visitor etiquette, you contribute to preserving this artistic marvel for generations to come.

3.3 St. Peter's Basilica

St. Peter's Basilica, a towering masterpiece of Renaissance architecture, is not only a symbol of religious devotion but also a testament to the artistic genius of renowned architects, including Michelangelo, Gian Lorenzo Bernini, and Carlo Maderno.

1. Architectural Marvel:
   - Designed by Michelangelo, Gian Lorenzo Bernini, and Carlo Maderno, St. Peter's Basilica combines Renaissance and Baroque elements, creating a harmonious blend of grandeur and grace.
   - The massive dome, designed by Michelangelo, stands as a crowning achievement, offering a symbol of heaven reaching down to Earth. Its iconic silhouette graces the skyline of Rome.
2. Altar and Baldachin:
   - The high altar, located directly above the tomb of St. Peter, is adorned with Gian Lorenzo Bernini's masterpiece, the Baldachin. This ornate bronze canopy serves as a visual

Chapter 4
Trastevere and the Tiber River

4.1 Exploring Trastevere

Nestled on the west bank of the Tiber River, Trastevere stands as a testament to the timeless charm of Rome. As you step into its labyrinthine streets, a unique atmosphere envelops you, blending historic allure with a distinct local vibe.

1. Cobblestone Alleys and Hidden Gems:
    *   Trastevere's narrow cobblestone alleys lead you on a journey through the heart of Rome's medieval past. Wander aimlessly, and you'll discover hidden piazzas, ancient fountains, and colorful facades that evoke the authentic spirit of the neighborhood.
2. Local Artisans and Boutiques:
    *   Embrace the bohemian ambiance as you encounter local artisans and boutiques showcasing handmade crafts. From unique jewelry to bespoke leather goods, Trastevere invites you to explore its thriving arts scene.
3. Piazzas and Gathering Spots:

- Piazzas such as Piazza Santa Maria in Trastevere serve as communal hubs where locals and visitors converge. Enjoy a moment of tranquility amidst the vibrant energy, surrounded by historic churches and charming cafes.
4. Street Performers and Music:
   - Trastevere often comes alive with the melodies of street performers and musicians. Whether it's the soulful notes of a guitar or the lively tunes of a street band, the musical backdrop adds a layer of enchantment to your exploration.

Best Eateries and Cafes:

1. Da Enzo al 29:
   - Known for its authentic Roman cuisine, Da Enzo al 29 offers classic dishes in a cozy, family-run setting. Indulge in pasta cacio e pepe or Roman-style artichokes for a truly local culinary experience.
2. Antico Forno La Renella:
   - A beloved bakery, Antico Forno La Renella entices with the aroma of freshly baked bread and an array of delectable pastries. Grab a slice of pizza bianca or a sweet treat to savor as you explore the streets.
3. Dar Poeta:
   - If you're in the mood for pizza, Dar Poeta is a Trastevere institution. With its wood-fired oven and diverse toppings, it offers a perfect blend of crispiness and flavor, attracting both locals and discerning pizza enthusiasts.
4. Caffè Sant'Eustachio:
   - Venture beyond Trastevere's borders to Caffè Sant'Eustachio for a taste of exceptional coffee. This historic cafe, renowned for its unique coffee blend, provides an ideal respite during your Roman exploration.
5. Freni e Frizioni:
   - As the sun sets, Freni e Frizioni emerges as a trendy spot for aperitivo. Enjoy a refreshing cocktail and an array of appetizers in this stylish former mechanic's shop turned hip bar.
6. Gelateria Fior di Luna:

- Conclude your Trastevere culinary adventure with a visit to Gelateria Fior di Luna. Indulge in artisanal gelato crafted from high-quality ingredients, with inventive flavors that reflect the creativity of Roman gelato artisans.

Trastevere, with its timeless allure and gastronomic treasures, invites you to savor the essence of Rome. As you stroll through its winding streets and relish the flavors of local eateries, you'll discover a neighborhood that seamlessly blends history, culture, and the warmth of Roman hospitality.

4.2 Tiber Island

Nestled in the Tiber River's gentle embrace, Tiber Island emerges as a captivating gem, weaving together a tapestry of history, legend, and healing. Its roots extend deep into the annals of Rome's past, making it a must-visit destination for those seeking a blend of serenity and historical richness.

1. Ancient Myths and Legends:
   - According to Roman mythology, Tiber Island is linked to the healing god Aesculapius. Legend has it that a sacred serpent, representing the god's presence, once resided on the island. This association with healing sanctuaries adds an enchanting layer to the island's allure.
2. Roman Bridges and Architecture:
   - Connected to both banks of the Tiber River by ancient bridges, Tiber Island is a testament to Roman engineering. The Fabricius Bridge, dating back to 62 BC, and the Ponte Cestio, built in the 1st century BC, provide picturesque passages to the island.
3. Hospital of San Giovanni Calibita:
   - The island has long been associated with healthcare. The Hospital of San Giovanni Calibita, founded in the 16th century, continues this legacy. While its medical role has evolved, the hospital's presence underscores Tiber Island's enduring connection to healing practices.

Unique Attractions:

1. Basilica of Saint Bartholomew on the Island:
   - A spiritual beacon on Tiber Island, the Basilica of Saint Bartholomew on the Island boasts a rich history. Originally founded in the 10th century, the basilica houses relics of Saint Bartholomew and serves as a sanctuary of peace and reflection.
2. Aventine Keyhole:
   - Venture to the Aventine Hill for a unique view of Tiber Island. Peering through the famed Aventine Keyhole at the Priory of the Knights of Malta, visitors are treated to a perfectly framed glimpse of the island, creating a captivating visual tableau.
3. Boat-Shaped Fountain:
   - Adorning Tiber Island is a charming boat-shaped fountain, a delightful feature that adds to the island's ambiance. The sound of flowing water complements the serene surroundings, creating a tranquil retreat in the heart of the city.
4. Isola Tiberina Film Festival:
   - Tiber Island's enchanting ambiance occasionally hosts cultural events. The Isola Tiberina Film Festival, held in the summer, transforms the island into an open-air cinema, providing a unique cinematic experience under the stars.
5. Tiberina Summer Festival:
   - Embrace the lively atmosphere during the Tiberina Summer Festival, featuring concerts, performances, and cultural events. This celebration adds a contemporary flair to the island's historical backdrop, inviting locals and visitors alike to partake in its vibrancy.

Tiber Island, with its rich historical tapestry and unique attractions, beckons explorers to delve into the layers of Roman lore and contemporary charm. As you traverse its ancient bridges, explore the basilica, and bask in the tranquility of its surroundings, Tiber Island unfolds as a timeless sanctuary in the heart of Rome.

4.3 Ponte Sisto

Ponte Sisto, an architectural marvel spanning the Tiber River, serves as a poetic link between the bohemian charm of Trastevere and the historic heart of Rome. This iconic bridge, steeped in history, invites travelers to embark on a visual journey that seamlessly merges the old and the new.

1. Ancient Origins and Renaissance Refinement:
    *   Originally constructed in the late 15th century during the Renaissance, Ponte Sisto replaced a crumbling medieval bridge. Its creation was commissioned by Pope Sixtus IV, hence the bridge's name, and it stands as a testament to the era's architectural prowess.
2. Traversing the Tiber in Style:
    *   Ponte Sisto's design embodies the Renaissance spirit, featuring elegant arches and balustrades. As you stroll across this historic span, you're met with panoramic views of the Tiber River, providing a timeless connection between Trastevere and the city center.
3. Statues of Saint Peter and Saint Paul:
    *   Two magnificent statues of Saint Peter and Saint Paul guard the bridge, adding a sacred dimension to its historical significance. These statues, positioned at either end, symbolize the spiritual journey undertaken by those who traverse Ponte Sisto.

Romantic Views:

1. Sunset Splendor:
    *   Ponte Sisto is renowned for offering one of the most enchanting views of Rome, especially during sunset. As the sun dips below the horizon, the warm hues cast a romantic glow over the cityscape, transforming the experience into a visual symphony.
2. City Lights and River Reflections:
    *   After nightfall, Ponte Sisto becomes a captivating vantage point for admiring Rome's illuminated skyline. The city

lights dance on the tranquil waters of the Tiber, creating a mesmerizing reflection that amplifies the romantic ambiance.

3. Riverbank Strolls:
    *   The areas surrounding Ponte Sisto invite couples and wanderers alike to enjoy leisurely strolls along the riverbanks. The gentle murmur of the Tiber and the soft glow of lampposts create an intimate setting, making it a favorite spot for romantic rendezvous.
4. Photographic Serenity:
    *   Photographers and admirers of visual poetry find Ponte Sisto an ideal subject. Whether capturing the bridge's silhouette against the twilight sky or framing the city's landmarks in the background, the bridge offers countless opportunities for creating lasting memories.
5. Cafés and Piazzas:
    *   Nearby cafés and charming piazzas provide perfect settings for sipping a cappuccino or enjoying a gelato while savoring the views. Ponte Sisto, with its timeless allure, becomes a backdrop for romantic interludes and serene moments.

Ponte Sisto, with its architectural grace and panoramic allure, transcends its role as a mere bridge. It becomes a symbol of connection, both physical and emotional, drawing lovers, explorers, and dreamers into its embrace. As you traverse this timeless span, allow the romantic views and historical resonance to weave a tale of love and wonder in the heart of Rome.

4.4 Tiber River Cruises

Embarking on a Tiber River cruise unveils a unique perspective of Rome's timeless beauty, and as the sun dips below the cityscape, the experience becomes a symphony of colors and history.

1. Sunset Splendor:
    *   Opting for a sunset cruise along the Tiber River is a magical way to witness Rome transform under the warm hues of the setting sun. The iconic landmarks, including St. Peter's Basilica, Castel Sant'Angelo, and Ponte Sant'Angelo, take on

Chapter 5
Roman Cuisine and Culinary Adventures

5.1 Traditional Roman Dishes

Embarking on a gastronomic journey in Rome means delving into the heart of traditional Roman dishes, where each bite is a celebration of time-honored recipes and local flavors.

1. Cacio e Pepe:
   - A simple yet exquisite pasta dish, Cacio e Pepe, translates to "cheese and pepper." The creamy sauce is made by combining Pecorino Romano cheese and black pepper with al dente pasta, resulting in a flavorful and comforting classic.
2. Carbonara:

- Carbonara is a beloved pasta dish featuring spaghetti, guanciale (cured pork cheek), eggs, Pecorino Romano cheese, and black pepper. The result is a rich, creamy, and indulgent flavor profile that captures the essence of Roman cuisine.

3. Amatriciana:
   - This pasta dish hails from the town of Amatrice, near Rome, and features a savory tomato sauce with cured pork jowl (guanciale) and Pecorino Romano cheese. Often paired with bucatini or rigatoni, Amatriciana embodies the robust flavors of Roman culinary heritage.

4. Supplì:
   - As a popular Roman street food, Supplì are deep-fried rice croquettes filled with ragù (meat sauce), tomato, and melted mozzarella. The crispy exterior and gooey, flavorful interior make them an irresistible snack.

5. Pizza Romana:
   - While pizza originated in Naples, Rome boasts its own version. Roman pizza is characterized by a thin, crispy crust and is often topped with classic combinations such as Margherita (tomato, mozzarella, and basil) or Marinara (tomato, garlic, oregano, and olive oil).

6. Saltimbocca alla Romana:
   - Saltimbocca alla Romana showcases tender veal slices enveloped in prosciutto and sage, pan-seared to perfection. The dish is often finished with a white wine and butter sauce, creating a savory and aromatic masterpiece.

7. Artichokes Roman-style (Carciofi alla Romana):
   - Romans have mastered the art of preparing artichokes, and Carciofi alla Romana is a testament to their culinary prowess. Artichokes are slow-cooked with garlic, mint, and parsley until tender, resulting in a dish that perfectly captures the flavors of spring.

Recommended Restaurants:

1. Da Enzo al 29:

- Located in Trastevere, Da Enzo al 29 is renowned for its authentic Roman cuisine. Indulge in classic dishes like Cacio e Pepe and Amatriciana in a cozy, family-run atmosphere.
2. Roscioli:
   - Nestled in the heart of Rome, Roscioli offers a gastronomic journey with a selection of traditional dishes. Their carbonara is particularly praised, and the restaurant's commitment to quality ingredients shines through in every dish.
3. Armando al Pantheon:
   - A stone's throw from the Pantheon, Armando al Pantheon is a historic eatery that serves traditional Roman fare. From Saltimbocca alla Romana to classic pasta dishes, the menu reflects the essence of Roman culinary traditions.
4. Pizzarium Bonci:
   - For an innovative take on Roman pizza, Pizzarium Bonci is a must-visit. This renowned pizzeria, founded by Gabriele Bonci, offers a variety of gourmet pizza slices with inventive toppings.
5. Il Goccetto:
   - If you're seeking a cozy enoteca to pair your Roman dishes with excellent wines, Il Goccetto is an ideal choice. This wine bar, tucked away in a charming alley, provides a relaxed atmosphere to savor local flavors.
6. Da Felice:
   - Situated in the Testaccio neighborhood, Da Felice is a historic trattoria serving Roman classics. From pasta dishes to hearty meat-based specialties, the restaurant exudes a warm and welcoming ambiance.

Embark on a culinary adventure through the streets of Rome, where each bite tells a story of tradition, passion, and the vibrant flavors that define Roman cuisine. Whether you opt for a cozy trattoria or an elegant ristorante, these recommended establishments promise an authentic taste of the Eternal City.

5.2 Food Markets

Nestled in the heart of Rome, Campo de' Fiori is not just a market; it's a vibrant tapestry of colors, scents, and flavors. This historic square transforms into a bustling market each morning, offering a sensory feast for both locals and visitors.

Fresh Produce and Local Flavors:

1. Colorful Market Stalls:
   - The lively market stalls at Campo de' Fiori burst with a kaleidoscope of colors, showcasing fresh fruits, vegetables, and vibrant flowers. Navigate through the cheerful chaos as vendors proudly display their seasonal produce.
2. Authentic Roman Ingredients:
   - Campo de' Fiori is a treasure trove of authentic Roman ingredients. From plump tomatoes and fragrant basil to regional cheeses and cured meats, the market provides the building blocks for crafting traditional Roman dishes in your own kitchen.
3. Delis and Specialty Shops:
   - Beyond fresh produce, the market is home to delis and specialty shops offering a variety of olive oils, balsamic vinegars, and condiments. Engage with the knowledgeable vendors to discover the nuances of these local culinary treasures.
4. Bakeries and Sweets:
   - Satisfy your sweet tooth with a visit to the bakeries and pastry stalls. Indulge in freshly baked bread, pastries, and biscotti that encapsulate the essence of Italian craftsmanship and culinary heritage.

Testaccio:

Overview: Testaccio, a neighborhood celebrated for its culinary heritage, hosts a market that mirrors the authentic and unpretentious spirit of Roman gastronomy. The Testaccio Market is a culinary haven where locals gather to procure fresh ingredients and relish the flavors of Rome.

Fresh Produce and Local Flavors:

1. Abundance of Fresh Seafood:
   - One of the highlights of Testaccio Market is its seafood section, where an abundance of fresh catches from the Mediterranean beckon seafood enthusiasts. From succulent shrimp to octopus and clams, the market offers an array of choices for creating seafood delicacies.
2. Meat and Cured Delights:
   - Testaccio Market is renowned for its meat and cured meat offerings. Explore stalls filled with prosciutto, salami, and regional specialties. Engage with the butchers to discover cuts ideal for traditional Roman recipes like amatriciana or carbonara.
3. Cheese and Dairy Delights:
   - The market's cheese and dairy section presents an assortment of Italian cheeses, both fresh and aged. Whether you're seeking creamy mozzarella for a Caprese salad or robust Pecorino for your pasta, Testaccio Market delivers.
4. Regional Wines and Liquors:
   - Elevate your culinary experience by exploring the market's wine and liquor section. Discover regional wines, artisanal spirits, and liqueurs that complement the rich flavors of Roman cuisine.

Culinary Experiences Beyond Shopping:

1. Street Food Stands:
   - Testaccio Market isn't just about ingredients; it's a destination for food experiences. Street food stands within the market offer a chance to savor Roman delicacies on the spot. From supplì to porchetta sandwiches, indulge in authentic flavors.
2. Cooking Classes and Demonstrations:
   - Some vendors at Testaccio Market offer cooking classes and demonstrations, allowing you to glean insights into the art of Roman cuisine. Learn the secrets of crafting pasta, sauces, and other culinary masterpieces from local experts.

Visiting Campo de' Fiori and Testaccio Markets immerses you in the heart and soul of Roman gastronomy. Whether you're a seasoned chef seeking premium ingredients or a curious traveler eager to taste the local flavors, these markets promise an enriching culinary experience in the Eternal City.

5.3 Wine Tasting in Rome

Rome, a city steeped in history and culinary excellence, invites you to embark on a journey through its enchanting wine culture. From intimate wine bars tucked away in cobblestone alleys to guided tours through the picturesque vineyards surrounding the Eternal City, Rome offers a diverse and rich tapestry for wine enthusiasts. Immerse yourself in the world of Italian wines as we explore esteemed wine bars and suggest captivating tours that unveil the elegance of Italian viticulture.

Italian Wines and Wine Bars:

1. Enoteca Antica:
   - A hidden gem in Trastevere, Enoteca Antica beckons with its cozy ambiance and a curated selection of Italian wines. This wine bar, embraced by the charm of the neighborhood, provides an intimate setting to savor the nuances of both renowned and lesser-known Italian varietals.
2. Il Goccetto:
   - Nestled near Campo de' Fiori, Il Goccetto stands as a testament to time, exuding Old-World charm. Delight in a vast array of wines available by the glass, inviting you to explore the diverse landscapes of Italian viticulture. The intimate atmosphere ensures a relaxed and educational wine-tasting experience.
3. Litro:
   - In the Monteverde neighborhood, Litro presents a modern twist on the traditional enoteca. Specializing in natural and organic wines, Litro allows you to embark on a journey of discovery. Pair your chosen wine with delectable small plates for a sensory exploration of Italian flavors.
4. Roscioli Salumeria con Cucina:

- A culinary haven in the heart of Rome, Roscioli Salumeria con Cucina marries exceptional dishes with an extensive wine list. Dive into the world of Italian wines, pairing them with expertly crafted dishes that showcase the synergy between food and wine in the Roman culinary tradition.

Wine Tour Suggestions:

1. Rome Wine Tours:
   - Engage in a guided wine tour through Rome's enotecas, led by experts who unveil the city's wine culture. This immersive experience introduces you to renowned Italian wines while providing fascinating insights into the stories behind each vineyard.
2. Frascati Wine Tour:
   - Venture beyond Rome to the charming town of Frascati, renowned for its exceptional white wines. A guided tour of Frascati's vineyards offers the chance to savor regional specialties while basking in the picturesque landscapes of the Roman countryside.
3. Trastevere Wine Walk:
   - Embark on a self-guided wine walk through the enchanting streets of Trastevere. This bohemian neighborhood, adorned with cobblestone paths, hosts numerous enotecas and wine bars. Sample regional wines while immersing yourself in the authentic Roman ambiance.
4. Wine Tasting in Castelli Romani:
   - Explore the historic towns of the Castelli Romani, just outside Rome, on a guided wine tour. Discover the renowned wines of Frascati, Marino, and Castel Gandolfo while enjoying the scenic beauty of these hilltop communities.
5. Lazio Wine Experience:
   - Immerse yourself in the wines of the Lazio region with a guided wine experience. Venture into the countryside surrounding Rome to explore lesser-known gems, visiting

vineyards and wineries that showcase the diversity of Lazio's viticultural landscape.

As you raise your glass in Rome, let the city's wine bars and tours be your guides through the exquisite world of Italian viticulture. Whether you seek the coziness of a traditional enoteca or the panoramic views of a countryside vineyard, Rome's wine scene promises an unforgettable journey through the refined elegance of Italian wines.

5.4 Gelato Hotspots

In the labyrinthine streets of Rome, where history and flavor intertwine, gelato stands as an irresistible emblem of culinary delight. The city, known for its rich gastronomic heritage, boasts gelaterias that elevate the art of frozen confections. Join us as we explore the best gelato hotspots in Rome, offering a palette of flavors that beckon both the discerning epicurean and the casual seeker of sweetness.

Best Gelaterias in the City:

1. Gelateria Fatamorgana:
    - Tucked away in Trastevere, Gelateria Fatamorgana is a haven for gelato enthusiasts seeking inventive flavors crafted with natural and organic ingredients. From classic favorites to avant-garde creations, each scoop is a testament to the gelateria's commitment to quality and creativity.
2. Giolitti:
    - Steeped in history, Giolitti is a legendary gelateria near the Pantheon that has been serving gelato since 1900. With an array of traditional and seasonal flavors, Giolitti invites you to savor the timeless allure of Rome while enjoying a cone amidst the city's historic splendor.
3. Il Gelato di San Crispino:
    - Il Gelato di San Crispino, located near the Trevi Fountain, is celebrated for its artisanal approach to gelato. Famed for its no-frills presentation and emphasis on pure, unadulterated

Chapter 6
Rome's Art and Culture Scene

6.1 Galleria Borghese

Nestled within the lush surroundings of Villa Borghese, Galleria Borghese stands as a testament to the splendor of Renaissance and Baroque art. This cultural gem in the heart of Rome beckons art enthusiasts and history aficionados alike, offering a mesmerizing journey through the works of masters from centuries past. Let's delve into the riches that Galleria Borghese holds and gather essential tips for an enriching visit.

Renaissance and Baroque Art Collection:

1. Bernini's Sculptures:
    • Galleria Borghese is renowned for its impressive collection of sculptures by Gian Lorenzo Bernini, one of the foremost

Baroque artists. Marvel at masterpieces like "Apollo and Daphne" and "David," where the sculptor's skill brings marble to life, capturing fleeting moments of emotion and movement.

2. Caravaggio's Paintings:
   - The gallery houses several works by the celebrated Baroque painter Caravaggio. His chiaroscuro technique and dramatic storytelling come to life in pieces such as "David with the Head of Goliath" and "Boy with a Basket of Fruit," leaving an indelible mark on the observer.

3. Titian, Raphael, and Correggio:
   - Galleria Borghese's extensive collection extends to Renaissance masters, including Titian, Raphael, and Correggio. Admire the delicate beauty of Titian's "Sacred and Profane Love," Raphael's "Lady with a Unicorn," and Correggio's luminous "Danaë," each contributing to the rich tapestry of artistic excellence.

4. Canova's Sculptures:
   - Antonio Canova's neoclassical sculptures add another layer of artistic brilliance to the collection. "Pauline Bonaparte as Venus Victrix" and "Apollo and Daphne" showcase Canova's mastery in portraying grace, beauty, and emotion.

Reservations and Visitor Tips:

1. Reservation Essential:
   - Due to the gallery's popularity and limited daily admissions, it is highly advisable to make reservations in advance. Booking a specific time slot ensures a more intimate and enjoyable experience amid the masterpieces.

2. Guided Tours:
   - Consider joining a guided tour to gain deeper insights into the artworks and their historical context. Knowledgeable guides provide fascinating narratives, enhancing your understanding of the artistic significance within Galleria Borghese.

3. Time Limitations:
   - Keep in mind that visitors are allotted a specific time window for their visit (usually two hours). This limitation is

ancient lineage and the enduring legacy of its visionary creator.

3. Interior Splendors:
   - Step into the vast interior of The Pantheon, where the harmony of proportions and the interplay of light and shadow create a transcendent atmosphere. Marvel at the intricate details of the coffered dome, adorned with rosettes, and appreciate the simplicity of the elegant marble interior.

4. Altar and Christian Additions:
   - The Pantheon's adaptation into a church introduced Christian elements while preserving the temple's classical features. An altar now graces the center of the space, and chapels dedicated to Christian saints line the periphery. The coexistence of ancient and Christian elements is a testament to the building's multifaceted history.

5. Tombs of the Illustrious:
   - The Pantheon serves as the final resting place for some of Italy's most revered figures, including the artist Raphael and the first two kings of a united Italy. Their tombs add a layer of historical and cultural significance to this already extraordinary monument.

Visitor Tips:

1. Time Your Visit:
   - Visit The Pantheon during daylight hours to fully appreciate the interplay of light through the oculus. An early morning or late afternoon visit provides a captivating play of sunlight within the interior.

2. Respectful Attire:
   - As The Pantheon functions as a church, visitors are encouraged to dress modestly and respectfully. This includes covering shoulders and knees.

3. Free Entry:
   - Entry to The Pantheon is free, making it an accessible and enriching experience for all visitors. Consider joining a guided tour to gain deeper insights into the history and architectural marvels of this iconic monument.

4. Piazza della Rotonda:

- After exploring The Pantheon, linger in the adjacent Piazza della Rotonda. Enjoy a coffee at one of the charming cafes and soak in the lively atmosphere of this historic square.

The Pantheon stands as a bridge across the centuries, inviting visitors to traverse the realms of ancient paganism and Christian worship. Its enduring magnificence continues to captivate, making it a must-visit destination for those seeking a profound connection to Rome's rich history and architectural legacy.

6.4 Contemporary Art Galleries

Rome, a city steeped in ancient history, also boasts a vibrant contemporary art scene. For those seeking to engage with the modern artistic pulse of the city, a journey through its contemporary art galleries is a must. Discover the dynamic and innovative expressions of Rome's artistic community, where tradition meets the avant-garde in a compelling dance of creativity.

Notable Galleries to Visit:

1. MACRO - Museo d'Arte Contemporanea Roma:
   - Located in the Salario-Nomentano district, MACRO is a powerhouse of contemporary art. The museum occupies two venues, MACRO Via Nizza and MACRO Testaccio, each offering a diverse range of exhibitions, installations, and performances. Explore cutting-edge works by both Italian and international artists in these expansive spaces dedicated to the contemporary arts.
2. MAXXI Arte - National Museum of 21st Century Arts:
   - While MAXXI is renowned for its architectural brilliance, it also houses an impressive collection of contemporary art. The museum hosts temporary exhibitions that push the boundaries of artistic expression. MAXXI Arte contributes to Rome's modern art landscape by fostering dialogues on contemporary issues through the lens of art.
3. Galleria Lorcan O'Neill:
   - Situated in the heart of Trastevere, Galleria Lorcan O'Neill is a beacon for contemporary art enthusiasts. The gallery

represents a diverse roster of international artists working across various mediums. With a commitment to supporting emerging talents, Galleria Lorcan O'Neill is a hub for artistic experimentation and exploration.

4. Gagosian Rome:
   - Gagosian, a renowned international gallery, has a presence in Rome. Located near Piazza del Popolo, Gagosian Rome showcases works by leading contemporary artists. The gallery's exhibitions often resonate with global art trends, providing a window into the broader landscape of contemporary art.

5. Rome Contemporary Art Fair (RomeArtWeek):
   - While not a specific gallery, RomeArtWeek is an annual event that transforms the entire city into a canvas for contemporary art. Galleries, studios, and cultural spaces open their doors to the public, offering a unique opportunity to engage directly with artists and witness the city's dynamic and diverse contemporary art scene.

6. Lorcan O'Neill Roma:
   - A sister gallery to Galleria Lorcan O'Neill, Lorcan O'Neill Roma is located in the Monti district. This intimate space showcases contemporary art exhibitions that reflect the gallery's commitment to presenting innovative and thought-provoking works.

7. Wunderkammern:
   - Wunderkammern, situated in the Ostiense neighborhood, is a contemporary art gallery that often blurs the lines between street art and gallery exhibitions. Known for promoting urban art, the gallery provides a platform for both established and emerging street artists, contributing to the city's vibrant visual landscape.

Visitor Tips:

1. Check Exhibition Schedules:
   - The contemporary art scene is dynamic, with exhibitions changing regularly. Check the schedules of the galleries you plan to visit to ensure you catch the latest and most relevant shows.

2. Participate in Art Events:
   - Keep an eye on art events and fairs happening in the city, such as RomeArtWeek. These events offer a comprehensive view of Rome's contemporary art community and provide opportunities to engage directly with artists.
3. Explore Different Districts:
   - Rome's contemporary art galleries are dispersed across various districts. Take the opportunity to explore different neighborhoods, each with its unique character, as you navigate the city's modern art scene.
4. Engage with Gallery Staff:
   - Gallery staff are often passionate about the art they represent. Don't hesitate to engage with them, ask questions, and gain insights into the artists and exhibitions on display.

As you navigate Rome's contemporary art landscape, you'll discover a city that embraces both its historical legacy and its vibrant, ever-evolving artistic spirit. From museum spaces to independent galleries, each venue contributes to the rich tapestry of Rome's modern artistic expression.

6.5 Street Art in Rome

Rome's ancient streets, adorned with centuries of history, also serve as a canvas for modern urban expression. Street art in the city breathes new life into its neighborhoods, offering a contemporary counterpoint to the classical backdrop. Explore the vibrant world of graffiti and murals, where the streets themselves become galleries for the dynamic and ever-evolving art scene.

Self-Guided Street Art Tours:

1. Ostiense District:
   - Begin your exploration in the Ostiense district, where industrial spaces and old factories provide a backdrop for bold and eclectic street art. Murals here often reflect the neighborhood's transformation into a hub for contemporary culture.
2. Testaccio:

- Adjacent to Ostiense, Testaccio boasts its own collection of street art gems. Wander through its streets to discover colorful murals that engage with both the urban environment and the community's history.
3. Quartiere Coppedè:
   - Quartiere Coppedè, known for its eclectic architecture, surprises visitors with unexpected street art installations. Stroll through this whimsical neighborhood to encounter a blend of classical and contemporary artistic expressions.
4. Pigneto:
   - Pigneto, a bohemian neighborhood, invites you to explore its street art while savoring the local atmosphere. The murals here often reflect the neighborhood's creative spirit and its status as a cultural melting pot.
5. San Lorenzo:
   - San Lorenzo, a student and artist quarter, is home to a diverse array of street art. From large murals to hidden gems, the neighborhood showcases the dynamic energy of Rome's contemporary art scene.

Tips for a Self-Guided Tour:

1. Local Guidance:
   - Engage with locals to get insights into the best street art spots. Locals often have a deep appreciation for the art in their neighborhoods and can provide valuable recommendations.
2. Explore Backstreets:
   - Don't limit your exploration to main streets. Some of the most captivating street art is tucked away in alleys and hidden corners, waiting to be discovered by the curious wanderer.
3. Capture the Moment:
   - Street art is transient, with new pieces often replacing old ones. Capture your favorite artworks with photographs, creating a personal record of your journey through Rome's urban art landscape.
4. Respect the Art and Environment:

- While street art is a form of public expression, it's essential to respect both the artists and the environment. Avoid damaging or defacing artworks, and be mindful of the neighborhoods you explore.
5. Adapt to Change:
   - Street art is dynamic, and new pieces may appear while others fade away. Embrace the ever-changing nature of the urban landscape, allowing each visit to be a unique experience.
6. Combine with Local Cuisine:
   - Pair your street art exploration with a culinary adventure. Many neighborhoods known for street art also boast diverse culinary scenes. Explore local cafes and eateries to make your journey a multisensory experience.

Rome's street art scene offers a fascinating juxtaposition to its historic treasures. As you traverse the city's neighborhoods adorned with vibrant murals and graffiti, you'll witness the fusion of ancient and modern, creating a unique tapestry that reflects Rome's multifaceted identity.

Chapter 7
Shopping and Fashion in Rome

7.1 Via Condotti

In the heart of Rome, Via Condotti stands as an illustrious thoroughfare, synonymous with luxury, opulence, and the epitome of high-end fashion. This iconic street, flanked by historic buildings and adorned with designer boutiques, invites fashion aficionados and discerning shoppers into a world where sophistication meets style. Let's embark on a journey through Via Condotti, where window shopping becomes an art form, and boutique finds are treasures of sartorial excellence.

High-End Fashion and Luxury Brands:

1. Gucci:
   - As you step onto Via Condotti, the double-G emblem of Gucci beckons. This flagship store is a haven for those seeking Italian luxury, featuring the latest fashion collections, accessories, and iconic pieces that embody the brand's distinctive style.
2. Valentino:
   - The red-carpet elegance of Valentino graces Via Condotti with a boutique that exudes timeless glamour. Discover

meticulously crafted couture, ready-to-wear masterpieces, and accessories that reflect the brand's commitment to sophistication and grace.

3. Bulgari:
   - A jewel in the crown of Via Condotti, Bulgari's flagship store showcases exquisite Italian craftsmanship in the form of stunning jewelry, watches, and accessories. The brand's distinctive style, inspired by Roman art and architecture, captivates those seeking unparalleled luxury.

4. Prada:
   - Prada's presence on Via Condotti is a testament to its avant-garde approach to fashion. Explore the boutique to discover cutting-edge designs, innovative materials, and accessories that redefine contemporary style.

5. Louis Vuitton:
   - The iconic monogram of Louis Vuitton graces Via Condotti with a sense of timeless elegance. This flagship store offers a curated selection of the brand's signature leather goods, fashion, and accessories, embodying the spirit of French luxury.

Window Shopping and Boutique Finds:

1. Antico Caffè Greco:
   - While not a fashion boutique, Antico Caffè Greco is a historic café that has been frequented by literary and artistic luminaries for centuries. Take a break from shopping to enjoy a coffee in this elegant setting, surrounded by artwork and the charm of old-world glamour.

2. Alberta Ferretti:
   - Alberta Ferretti's boutique on Via Condotti captures the essence of romantic and feminine elegance. Delicate fabrics, intricate embellishments, and flowing silhouettes define the brand's signature style, making it a destination for those seeking timeless sophistication.

3. Brunello Cucinelli:
   - Known for its commitment to ethical luxury, Brunello Cucinelli's boutique on Via Condotti offers a refined selection of cashmere clothing, tailored pieces, and

For those enchanted by the allure of the past and the stories embedded in time-worn treasures, Rome unveils a world of vintage and antique shops. Beyond the bustling modernity, these establishments are sanctuaries of history, offering collectors and enthusiasts a chance to uncover unique items that echo bygone eras. Let's embark on a journey through Rome's vintage and antique scene, where each shop is a portal to a different chapter of the city's rich history.

Hidden Gems for Collectors:

1. Antiquariato Valligiano:
   - Tucked away in the charming neighborhood of Trastevere, Antiquariato Valligiano is a haven for antique enthusiasts. This hidden gem is known for its diverse collection, featuring everything from vintage furniture to exquisite art pieces. Navigate through its curated aisles to discover timeless treasures.
2. Mercato Monti:
   - Mercato Monti, located near the Colosseum, transforms into a treasure trove of vintage finds on the weekends. This open-air market hosts a mix of local artisans and vintage sellers, offering a unique blend of antique items, retro fashion, and eclectic collectibles.
3. Antico Mercato Monti:
   - Not to be confused with the aforementioned Mercato Monti, Antico Mercato Monti is a permanent vintage market in the Monti district. Dive into its stalls to find a curated selection of vintage clothing, accessories, and home decor items that capture the spirit of yesteryears.
4. Borghetto Flaminio Market:
   - Held every Sunday near Piazza del Popolo, the Borghetto Flaminio Market is a sprawling marketplace featuring antiques, vintage fashion, and collectibles. Stroll through its aisles to uncover hidden gems and unique artifacts from different periods.
5. Antico Forno Roscioli:
   - While primarily a historic bakery, Antico Forno Roscioli in Campo de' Fiori conceals a secret. Behind the bakery, you'll

find a small vintage corner offering antique kitchenware, utensils, and unique culinary collectibles.

Where to Find Unique Items:

1. Federico Rivalta Vintage:
   - Situated near Piazza Navona, Federico Rivalta Vintage specializes in curated vintage clothing and accessories. Step into this boutique to find unique fashion pieces that evoke the elegance of bygone decades.
2. Soffitta Sotto i Portici:
   - Located in the charming district of Trastevere, Soffitta Sotto i Portici is a delightful vintage shop tucked beneath ancient porticos. Explore its carefully curated collection of vintage clothing, accessories, and retro home decor items.
3. King Size Vintage:
   - As the name suggests, King Size Vintage, near Termini Station, is a spacious vintage store offering a wide range of clothing, accessories, and decor items. From classic styles to bold retro fashion, this shop caters to diverse tastes.
4. Frip Roma:
   - Frip Roma, in the San Lorenzo district, is a thrift shop that draws in vintage enthusiasts seeking unique and affordable finds. Explore its racks for second-hand clothing, accessories, and eclectic pieces that embody the charm of vintage fashion.
5. Mad Vintage Roma:
   - Mad Vintage Roma, near Campo de' Fiori, is a popular spot for vintage and second-hand clothing. The shop's eclectic collection includes a mix of styles and eras, making it a go-to destination for those seeking distinctive wardrobe additions.

Tips for Vintage Shopping:

1. Explore Varied Districts:
   - Rome's vintage and antique shops are scattered across different districts. Explore diverse neighborhoods like

Trastevere, Monti, and San Lorenzo to discover unique items and soak in the local atmosphere.

2. Weekend Markets:
   - Weekends often bring vintage markets to life. Plan your visit to coincide with markets like Mercato Monti or Borghetto Flaminio for a diverse selection of antiques and collectibles.

3. Ask for Stories:
   - Engage with shop owners and sellers to learn the stories behind the items. Vintage shopping is not just about the objects; it's also about the narratives and histories they carry.

4. Keep an Open Mind:
   - Vintage shopping requires a spirit of exploration. Keep an open mind, and be prepared to discover unexpected treasures that may not conform to a specific era or style.

5. Inspect Quality:
   - When purchasing vintage items, carefully inspect their condition. Vintage pieces often bear signs of wear, but assessing their quality ensures that you bring home items that will endure.

Rome's vintage and antique shops offer a delightful escape into the past, where every item has a story to tell. As you navigate through these hidden gems, you'll find yourself immersed in the timeless charm of bygone eras, each purchase becoming a unique piece of the city's historical mosaic.

7.4 Roman Markets

Amidst the ancient streets of Rome, vibrant markets come to life, offering a sensory feast for visitors seeking unique treasures and authentic experiences. From bustling flea markets to stalls brimming with artisanal goods, Rome's markets are a reflection of the city's rich cultural tapestry. Let's explore the charm of Roman markets, where every stall tells a story and every purchase becomes a tangible memory of your time in the Eternal City.

Flea Markets and Artisanal Goods:

1. Porta Portese Market:

- Held every Sunday near Trastevere, Porta Portese is one of Rome's largest and most famous flea markets. It sprawls through the streets, offering a diverse array of goods, from vintage clothing and antiques to books and collectibles. Navigate through the lively atmosphere to uncover hidden gems and unique finds.

2. Campo de' Fiori Market:
   - Nestled in the heart of Rome, Campo de' Fiori hosts a bustling market in the morning, transforming the square into a colorful tapestry of fresh produce, flowers, and artisanal products. Explore the stalls to experience the vibrant energy of a traditional Roman market.

3. Mercato di Testaccio:
   - Testaccio's market is a food lover's paradise, offering an array of fresh produce, meats, cheeses, and more. Beyond culinary delights, the market also features stalls with clothing, accessories, and household items. Immerse yourself in the local atmosphere as you explore this dynamic market.

4. Mercato Monti:
   - While known for its vintage finds, Mercato Monti, near the Colosseum, also hosts a market showcasing contemporary artisanal goods. Browse through handmade jewelry, unique accessories, and creative artworks crafted by local designers.

5. Mercato Trionfale:
   - Located near the Vatican, Mercato Trionfale is a bustling market offering a wide variety of products, including fresh produce, cheeses, and gourmet delights. The market provides an authentic Roman shopping experience away from the tourist crowds.

Souvenir Shopping Tips:

1. Local Artisans:
   - Seek out stalls and shops featuring goods crafted by local artisans. Whether it's handmade jewelry, leather goods, or ceramics, supporting local artists ensures that your souvenirs carry a piece of authentic Roman craftsmanship.

2. Taste of Rome:

- Consider purchasing local delicacies as souvenirs. Olive oil, wine, pasta, and traditional sweets make for delightful gifts that capture the essence of Roman cuisine.
3. Unique Keepsakes:
   - Look for unique keepsakes that go beyond typical tourist trinkets. Handcrafted items, art prints, and locally designed goods offer a more personal and meaningful connection to your Roman experience.
4. Negotiate Thoughtfully:
   - While negotiating is common in markets, approach it with respect and thoughtfulness. Keep in mind that many vendors rely on their sales, and a fair transaction ensures a positive experience for both parties.
5. Local Markets vs. Tourist Areas:
   - Explore markets frequented by locals, as they often feature more authentic products at reasonable prices. While markets in tourist areas have their charm, venturing into neighborhood markets provides a deeper connection to Roman daily life.

Roman Market Etiquette:

1. Respect Personal Space:
   - Markets can get crowded, especially during peak hours. Respect personal space and be mindful of others as you navigate through the stalls.
2. Cash is King:
   - Many market vendors prefer cash transactions. Ensure you have sufficient cash on hand, especially for smaller purchases.
3. Ask Questions:
   - Engage with vendors, ask questions about their products, and learn about the stories behind the items. This interaction adds a layer of richness to your shopping experience.
4. BYOB (Bring Your Own Bag):
   - Consider bringing a reusable bag to carry your purchases. Not only is it eco-friendly, but it also makes it easier to navigate through the market.
5. Stay Hydrated:

- Markets can be bustling, and exploring under the sun can be tiring. Carry a water bottle to stay hydrated and energized during your market adventure.

Rome's markets are a treasure trove of experiences, offering a glimpse into the city's vibrant culture and diverse offerings. As you meander through the stalls, each interaction becomes a chance to connect with the artisans, taste local flavors, and bring home a piece of Rome that is uniquely yours.

7.5 Fashion Events and Festivals

Rome, a city renowned for its timeless sense of style, hosts an array of fashion events and festivals throughout the year, creating a dynamic tapestry of sartorial celebration. From haute couture showcases to emerging designer platforms, these events invite fashion enthusiasts to immerse themselves in the evolving trends and creative expressions of the Eternal City. Let's explore Rome's fashion calendar and provide attendees with a guide to navigating these stylish spectacles.

Rome's Fashion Calendar:

1. Altaroma:
   - Altaroma is Rome's premier fashion event, held biannually in January and July. This prestigious showcase brings together established designers, emerging talents, and industry insiders. Attendees can expect runway shows, presentations, and exhibitions that celebrate the intersection of tradition and innovation in Italian fashion.
2. Roma Fashion Week:
   - Roma Fashion Week, typically held in February and September, unfolds as a dynamic platform for both Italian and international designers. This event presents a diverse range of collections, from ready-to-wear to avant-garde creations, and offers a glimpse into the future of global fashion trends.
3. Rome Fashion Film Festival:

- The Rome Fashion Film Festival, usually scheduled in November, explores the symbiotic relationship between fashion and film. Attendees can enjoy screenings of fashion-inspired films, documentaries, and discussions that delve into the artistic convergence of these two creative realms.

4. Fashion Graduate Italia:
   - Celebrating the talents of emerging designers, Fashion Graduate Italia is an event that focuses on the work of recent graduates from prestigious fashion schools. Held in July, this platform provides a glimpse into the future of Italian fashion through the eyes of young visionaries.

5. Ethical Fashion Festival:
   - Promoting sustainability and ethical practices in the fashion industry, the Ethical Fashion Festival in Rome encourages dialogue on responsible fashion choices. Attendees can explore eco-friendly designs, attend discussions on ethical fashion, and engage with brands committed to positive environmental and social impact.

Attendees' Guide to Fashion Events:

1. Plan Ahead:
   - Fashion events often have specific schedules and locations. Plan your attendance in advance, noting the dates, venues, and any special events or exhibitions that may interest you.

2. Ticketing and Registration:
   - Check the event's official website for information on ticketing and registration. Some fashion events may require advance booking or have limited availability for certain shows.

3. Dress the Part:
   - Embrace the opportunity to showcase your personal style. Fashion events are an excellent occasion to express yourself through clothing, so don your most stylish ensemble and be part of the fashion-forward crowd.

4. Network and Socialize:
   - Fashion events are not only about the runway; they're also networking opportunities. Engage with fellow attendees,

designers, and industry professionals. Attend after-parties or networking events associated with the fashion calendar.

5. Stay Informed:
    - Keep yourself updated on any changes or additions to the schedule. Follow the official social media accounts of the events and subscribe to newsletters for real-time updates and announcements.

6. Explore Surrounding Areas:
    - While attending fashion events, take the opportunity to explore the neighborhoods and districts where they are held. Rome's charm extends beyond the event venues, offering hidden gems and stylish boutiques to discover.

7. Capture the Moments:
    - Document your experience by taking photographs and sharing your highlights on social media. Many fashion events encourage attendee participation, and your unique perspective adds to the overall narrative of the event.

8. Respect Etiquette:
    - Familiarize yourself with any specific etiquette or guidelines for attendees. Some events may have dress codes or protocols that enhance the overall experience.

9. Attend Talks and Workshops:
    - Fashion events often include panel discussions, talks, and workshops. Take advantage of these opportunities to gain insights into the fashion industry, trends, and the creative process.

10. Support Emerging Designers:
    - Attend shows and presentations by emerging designers. These platforms are essential for nurturing new talent, and you might discover the next big name in fashion.

Rome's fashion events and festivals create a captivating narrative that merges tradition with innovation. Whether you're a fashion enthusiast, industry professional, or simply curious about the evolving world of style, attending these events in the Eternal City offers a front-row seat to the intersection of creativity, culture, and couture.

Conclusion
Practical Information and Final Thoughts

In the journey through the "Roma Travel Guide," we've explored the rich tapestry of Rome – its history, culture, landmarks, culinary delights, hidden gems, and vibrant fashion scene. As we conclude this guide, let's recap some practical information and share final thoughts to enhance your experience in the Eternal City.

Practical Information:

1. Transportation:
   - Rome boasts an extensive public transportation system, including buses, trams, and the metro. Consider purchasing a Roma Pass for convenient access to public transportation and cultural sites.
2. Currency and Language:
   - The official currency is the Euro (€), and Italian is the primary language. While English is widely understood in tourist areas, learning a few basic Italian phrases can enhance your interactions with locals.
3. Weather and Best Time to Visit:
   - Rome experiences a Mediterranean climate. The spring (April to June) and fall (September to October) are ideal for pleasant weather and fewer crowds. Summer can be hot, and winter brings cooler temperatures.
4. Local Customs and Etiquette:
   - Respect local customs, such as covering your shoulders when entering religious sites and greeting people with a friendly "Buongiorno" or "Buonasera." Tipping is not as common as in some other countries, but it's appreciated for exceptional service.
5. Dress Code and Security:
   - Dress modestly when visiting religious sites, and be mindful of dress codes in upscale establishments. Keep your belongings secure, especially in crowded areas, to prevent pickpocketing.
6. Shopping Tips:

- Explore diverse shopping districts, from the luxury boutiques on Via Condotti to the trendy finds in Campo Marzio. Negotiate thoughtfully in markets, and consider supporting local artisans for unique souvenirs.
7. Fashion Events and Festivals:
   - Check Rome's fashion calendar for events like Altaroma and Roma Fashion Week. Plan your attendance in advance, dress stylishly, and take advantage of networking opportunities.

Final Thoughts:

Rome, with its timeless allure and captivating history, offers a multifaceted experience for every traveler. Whether you're exploring the iconic Colosseum, savoring traditional Roman dishes, or immersing yourself in the city's fashion scene, Rome invites you to be part of its rich narrative.

As you navigate through the city's cobblestone streets, each step is a journey through centuries of art, culture, and the indomitable spirit of Rome. From the grandeur of the Vatican to the intimate charm of Trastevere, every corner reveals a story waiting to be discovered.

So, whether you're a history enthusiast, a food connoisseur, or a fashion aficionado, Rome welcomes you with open arms. Embrace the magic of the Eternal City, savor every moment, and let the essence of Rome linger in your memories long after you bid arrivederci. Buon viaggio!

Printed in Great Britain
by Amazon

38347491R00056